4⁹⁹

W9-BKS-567

THIS BOOK
BELONGS TO

....

....

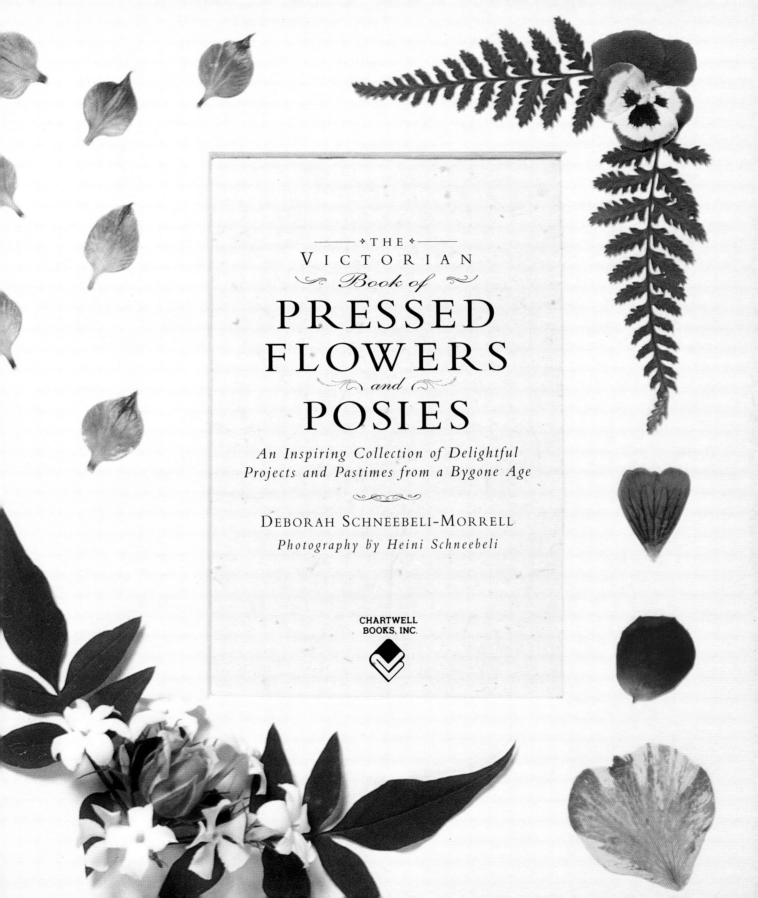

THE
VICTORIAN
Book of
PRESSED
FLOWERS
and
POSIES

*An Inspiring Collection of Delightful
Projects and Pastimes from a Bygone Age*

DEBORAH SCHNEEBELI-MORRELL

Photography by Heini Schneebeli

CHARTWELL
BOOKS, INC.

The Victorian Book of
Pressed Flowers and Posies

Designed and created by
THE BRIDGEWATER BOOK COMPANY LTD

Art Director: Peter Bridgewater
Designer: Jane Lanaway
Editor: Geraldine Christy
Managing Editor: Mandy Greenfield
Photography: Heini Schneebeli
Page makeup: Chris Lanaway

CHARTWELL BOOKS
A division of Book Sales, Inc.
114 Northfield Avenue
Edison, NJ 08837 USA

CLB 4085
© 1995 CLB Publishing, Godalming, Surrey
All rights reserved.
Color separation by HBM Print Ltd, Singapore
Printed and bound in Singapore by Tien Wah Press

ISBN 0-7858-0379-3

CONTENTS

INTRODUCTION
10

LEAFY LAMPSHADE
21

BOOKMARK AND GIFT TAGS
28

HYACINTHS AND GARLANDS
37

CANDLES
12

BEADED GLOVES
22

POTPOURRI
30

STENCILLED NOTEBOOK
38

VIOLETS AND PANSIES
14

PRESSED FLOWER PICTURE MOUNT
24

CRYSTALLIZED VIOLETS
32

HERB PILLOW
41

HEARTS
16

DÉCOUPAGE PICTURE FRAME
25

TEAPOT STAND
33

DRIED FLOWERS
42

INDEX
44

PRESSED FLOWER CARD AND PICTURE
18

GLASS FLOWERS
26

SHELL BOXES
34

ACKNOWLEDGMENTS
45

INTRODUCTION

❦

$\mathcal{T}$HE VICTORIANS were passionate about gardening. Botany was studied seriously in childhood, and pressing flowers was often the first craft a child would learn.

There was an abundance of books and journals published for the amateur gardener to keep up with this fervent interest in plants and the natural world. Women, in particular, avidly collected, pressed and assembled beautiful specimens from the garden into lovely floral albums enhanced by sentimental verse, watercolour painting and accomplished penmanship. Flowers, grasses, leaves and seed pods were picked, dried and arranged into all manner of baskets, vases and urns to grace the mantelpiece, drawing room, dining room or parlour, and were arranged into bouquets, sprays, wreaths, buttonholes and hair ornaments.

The all-pervasive flower motif was used extensively in embroidery. The beaded glove project on pages 22–3 uses exquisite little metal beads and sequins to create a sparkling posy on the backs of the gloves.

Making skeletonized leaves was another popular pastime, and pages 20–1 demonstrate a way of using them to decorate a lampshade. This is surprisingly easy to do and there is something quite magical about revealing the lacy vein structure of a leaf.

Artificial flowers were deftly created from wax, feathers, wool, silk and shells, and were made into permanent displays, some of which still survive. Glass domes, characteristic of the period, were placed over these to protect the fragile contents from being ravaged by the large amounts of coal dust produced from fires within the house. The project on pages 26–7 shows you how to make your own glass-domed dried-flower arrangement to put in pride of place in your home.

The stencilled fern leaf notebook on pages 38–9 is one of the simplest projects in the book to make and gives rewarding results. Once you have perfected the technique, try decorating other objects in the house such as picture frames, blanket chests or old cupboards.

All you need to press flowers successfully is a large heavy book and some sheets of absorbent paper to place your specimens between. Use them to prettify plain white candles, as shown on pages 12–13, or to decorate a personal Valentine you are sending (page 16) or to make a stunning picture of a basket of flowers (page 18).

Flowers were used in the kitchen as well and some flowers can be preserved in egg white and sugar. One of the most popular examples of these are crystallized violets (page 32), often used as decoration on delicious chocolate cakes.

CANDLES

*B*EFORE GAS for lighting was widely installed in Victorian homes, candles were used sparingly. The wax variety was generally only used in grander homes or when important guests were expected. Servants had to make do with tallow candles that smoked and sputtered uncontrollably. Candles were never left unattended and it was important to extinguish them at night to save the wax and protect the home from fire. Pressing flowers was a favourite activity of Victorian ladies, and here flowers are used to decorate candles. It only takes about two weeks to press flowers successfully. If you do not have a flower press just lay your specimens carefully between absorbent paper within the pages of a heavy book. When pressed, the following flowers and leaves are suitable for sticking onto candles: pansies, ferns, lavender, potentilla, primrose, hydrangeas, geranium and any pretty small leaves.

MATERIALS

Selection of dried flowers

Wax glue

Small double saucepan

Small paintbrush

Assortment of wax candles

Dipping can 8 × 20 cm (3 × 8 in)

1 kg (2 lb) paraffin wax

Deep saucepan

*J*ust a little candle, shining
in the dark,
Drives away the shadows with each tiny spark.

The Children's Friend
1895

1 Select the flowers you are going to use. If you decide to use leaves, make sure they are a little shorter than the candle.

2 Melt a small amount of the wax glue over hot water in a small double saucepan. With the small paintbrush put spots of glue onto the candle where the flowers will be placed. The glue dries quickly; press the flowers onto the candle while the glue is drying.

3 Continue gluing the flowers around the candle.

4 *Put the dipping can full of paraffin wax into a deep pan of very hot water. The wax will reduce as it melts.*

5 *Holding the candle by the wick, quickly dip it in and out of the hot wax; dip twice only so that the outer layer of wax is thin enough for the pressed flowers to show through.*

CAROL SERVICE

Many of the larger aristocratic country houses in England have their own adjoining private chapel. Here the servants were expected to attend family worship on Sunday. On Christmas Eve the entire household from above and below stairs, including any house guests present for the festivities, gathered for the candlelit carol service held in the late afternoon. This was a magical time for the occupants of the nursery quarters, especially if they had been involved in the decoration of the candles.

Candles were usually bought in with tea; but we only burnt one at a time. As we lived in constant preparation for a friend who might come in, any evening (but who never did), it required some contrivance to keep our candles of the same length, ready to be lighted, and to look as if we burnt two always.

Cranford
ELIZABETH GASKELL 1810–65

VIOLETS AND PANSIES

*V*IOLETS AND their close relatives, pansies and miniature violas, were particular favourites in the Victorian garden. The sweet violet is famous for its fragrance, which is used in perfumes, eau de Cologne and in scented pastilles to sweeten the breath. Pansies flower later than violets, their upturned smiling faces always a welcome sight at the front of a border. Pansies and violets are normally grown as biennials, but if the seeds are sown early enough they will flower later the same year.

TO GROW PANSIES FROM SEED

1 Sow the pansy seeds 1.5 mm ($^1/_{16}$ in) deep in good seed compost in early spring. Cover to exclude the light.

2 Keep the soil moist and fairly warm. Remove the cover when the seedlings appear.

3 Transplant the seedlings into trays spaced 5 cm (2 in) apart, when they are large enough to handle. Grow on in good light.

4 Acclimatize plants to the outside gradually and after ten days transplant to their final flowering positions. These flowers are happily suited to growing in pots.

TUSSIE MUSSIE

*T*he Tussie Mussie was a small, tightly bound hand-held posy of fragrant flowers. In the mid-nineteenth century it became popular as an accessory carried by fashionable ladies. When presented by an admirer it became a vehicle for the floral 'language of love' in which symbolic messages were carried by the inclusion of certain flowers. The pansy meant 'You are in my thoughts' and the violet stood for faithfulness. The herbs and flowers in this Tussie Mussie have been picked from an English cottage garden and include marigolds, feverfew, small roses, cornflowers and pinks.

1 Start with a small posy in the middle and encircle it with a variety of contrasting herbs and flowers. Bind together as you go along with a reel of fine florists' wire.

2 Gradually build up the Tussie Mussie, adding different flowers. Space them evenly according to colour; insert the leafy herbs amongst the flowers.

3 Encircle with an outer rim of small-leafed herbs like rosemary or santolina. Bind to finish, cut the stems evenly and push a posie holder up so the lacy edge touches the flowers.

*A violet by a mossy stone
Half hidden from the eye!
Fair as a star, when only one
Is shining in the sky*

WILLIAM WORDSWORTH
1770–1850

HEARTS

MANY VICTORIAN Valentines were extremely complicated; one dated 1846 showed a finely dressed gentleman whose waistcoat opened to reveal his heart, on which was a picture of his lady love. The family firm of Jonathan King was well known in the late 1800s for their highly decorated Valentines using wonderful combinations of tinsel, swansdown, glass beads, dried flowers and pressed ferns.

VALENTINE

The main image in this unusual Valentine is the pressed heart-shaped leaf from which a smaller heart motif has been cut. Many leaves are heart-shaped; violets are perfect, if a little small. Pick them with the stalk still attached and press between absorbent paper within the leaves of a heavy book.

MATERIALS

Pressed large heart-shaped leaf

Off-white handmade paper

Pinking shears

Deep purple card

Small scissors

Sharp soft pencil

Craft knife

Cutting mat

Small selection of pressed flowers and small ferns

Toothpicks for applying glue

Rubber-based glue for flowers

30 cm (12 in) of purple rayon ribbon 1 cm (½ in) wide

1 Lay the heart-shaped leaf on off-white paper and cut around it with pinking shears so that there is 3 cm (1¼ in) extra at the sides, base and top of the leaf. Cut the purple card 2 cm (¾ in) larger than the background paper.

2 Cut a small heart shape from the off-cuts of the off-white paper. Lay it onto the centre of the pressed leaf. Draw around it and cut it out with the craft knife; this should be done on a cutting mat.

3 Put the leaf in the centre of the paper and arrange the other pressed flowers in a circlet around it; stick them in place. Choose a small matching flower to fit inside the cut-out heart. Use the toothpicks to dab small amounts of glue onto the paper where the flowers are to be stuck. Allow the glue to dry.

4 Cut two small slits either side of the stalk of the leaf. Thread the ribbon through and tie into a pretty bow. Then glue the whole onto the purple card so that a narrow border is visible.

❧ LOVE NOTES ❧

With the magical use of a photocopier it is easy to make a pretty collection of charming notelets. Tied together in sets with an attractive ribbon, they make a really special gift for an important person. If you do not have any ivory paper you can achieve an antiqued effect by painting white paper with tea; allow it to dry, then iron out any crinkles with a medium hot iron.

MATERIALS

Selection of black and white engravings of flower posies and decorative borders

Scissors

Paper glue

2 A4 sheets of white paper

5 A4 sheets of ivory paper

Coloured ribbon

1 Select an appealing black and white engraving of flowers. Cut it out and paste it onto white A4 paper.

2 Cut out a border and frame this image; the frame should be about 11×8 cm (4½ × 3 in). Mitre the corners of the border.

3 Fold another piece of white A4 paper into four so that it opens on a long side like a card. Paste your posy and border onto the front quarter of the paper. Open out.

4 Using the ivory paper photocopy this A4 sheet 5 times. Fold the pieces of paper into notelets and tie together in a bundle with colourful ribbon.

𝒯his simple gift I wish to be a token of my love for thee.
VICTORIAN VALENTINE

MANY VICTORIAN women and children took a serious interest in flowers and made comprehensive collections of pressed flowers, leaves and even seaweed. They also used them for craftwork and it was common for specimens to be prettily arranged around hand-written verse. Others were made into charming pictures that were framed and displayed for all to admire. The one shown here is a lavish traditional display of pressed flowers bursting out of a fabulous fern basket.

PRESSED FLOWER PICTURE

MATERIALS

Scissors

Small piece of card

Paintbrush

Rubber-based glue for flowers

Pressed flowers, in differing shapes and sizes; leaves, ferns, grasses, moss and bracken fronds

Tweezers for handling flowers

Toothpicks

Handmade paper to fit frame

25 cm (10 in) square picture frame

1 Cut a basket shape from the card, paint glue over the surface and stick the moss tightly onto the card. Cut fern leaves and bracken fronds to required length and stick them over the moss to imitate a woven basket.

2 Stick the fern basket onto a piece of handmade paper approximately 18 × 20 cm (7 × 8 in) or to fit a ready-made frame.

3 Lay your flowers, leaves and grasses into the basket in a bouquet arrangement. When you are happy with your design, stick them in place. When the glue is dry, frame the finished picture.

PRESSED FLOWER CARD

You can buy ready-made cards, the front of which is an oval window mount. Suitable flowers for pressing are rosebay willow herb, cranesbill, geranium, potentillas, geums, statice and cistus.

MATERIALS

Single pressed flower (cistus) and selection of smaller ones

Absorbent paper

Tweezers for handling flowers

Piece of pink paper to fit behind oval window

Ready-made card with oval window mount

Pencil

Rubber-based glue for flowers

Paper glue

Toothpicks for applying the glue

Small scissors

White paper doilie

Wire-edged ribbon, colour chosen to match flower

1 Pick suitable flowers on a dry day. Carefully lay your specimens onto a folded sheet of absorbent paper. Fold over to enclose the flowers and place between the leaves of a heavy book. It takes about two weeks to press them successfully.

2 Slip the pink paper behind the oval opening of the card and trace the shape of the mount very faintly in pencil onto the backing paper where the flowers will be arranged.

3 Open out the card and arrange your flower design within the pencilled area. Place the large flower centrally and stick it down carefully, dabbing the glue under the flower petals.

4 Glue the small statice flowerheads around the oval facing inwards so that the stems will be hidden by the mount. When you are happy with the design close the card, gluing the backing paper to the back of the oval mount.

5 Cut out small sections of paper doilie, then arrange and glue them in position around the oval mount on the front of the card.

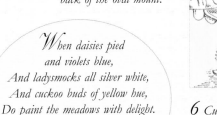

When daisies pied and violets blue, And ladysmocks all silver white, And cuckoo buds of yellow hue, Do paint the meadows with delight.

'Spring', Love's Labour's Lost
WILLIAM SHAKESPEARE
1564–1616

6 Cut two slits along the folded side, push the ribbon through and tie into a bow. Trim the ends at an angle.

LEAFY LAMPSHADE

*D*ELICATE SKELETONIZED leaves have been used to decorate this pretty lampshade. Use a plain paper shade so that the intricate veining of the leaves shows through to best effect when the lamp is lit. This shade is quick to make and creates an effective home accessory. Skeletonized willow leaves have been used here; they are commercially available from a good florist and are relatively inexpensive.

MATERIALS

Selection of skeletonized willow leaves
Ready-made natural paper lampshade
Paintbrush
Rubber-based glue

1 *Collect a variety of undamaged leaves in mid summer. Soak in a bowl of rainwater for about a month; this softens the leaf tissue.*

HOW TO SKELETONIZE LEAVES

'*R*eady made' skeletonized leaves are not hard to find; look carefully for them when you walk through woods. If you want a variety of shapes and perfect leaves with a predictable result, however, you need to make them yourself. Fleshy leaves are the best, and magnolia are particularly suitable.

1 *Try out the leaves against the lampshade, holding up one or two at a time to plan their positions. When you have decided on your design, brush the back of a leaf very thinly with the glue.*

2 *Put the leaf in position on the shade. As the leaves will be decorating a curved surface you will need to press each one securely. Continue sticking leaves evenly around the shade, leaving an even gap between each.*

2 *Take the leaves out of the rainwater and rinse them under cold water.*

3 *Brush them very gently with a soft brush to remove the cotton tissue from the delicate leaf veins. Allow to dry.*

4 *Iron them carefully and place them between the pages of a book to store them flat until needed for use.*

BEADED GLOVES

*I*T IS STILL possible to find exquisite examples of Victorian beadwork, often used to decorate purses, ladies' jackets, belts and all manner of accessories. Much patience was required to create the characteristic tightly packed designs and, as in all Victorian needlecrafts, the flower motif was very common. Tiny metal beads and sequins have been used to transform these rich green velour gloves into stunning evening wear.

MATERIALS

Pair of green velour gloves
Tailor's chalk
Selection of tiny metal beads
Needle
Dark green thread
Round, bronze-coloured sequins
Leaf-shaped sequins
4 pink flower sequins

1 Draw your design onto the back of each glove with the tailor's chalk. It is best to keep your design fairly simple.

2 Using some of the metal beads, sew each bead separately onto the glove, making a ring around the centre of the flower.

3 Sew the round sequins into the centre of the flower.

OPERA

*T*he young Princess Victoria during her austere and lonely childhood was taken to the opera and ballet as often as three times a week, and became infatuated with that exciting, emotional world. In her journal she records her youthful foray into theatre criticism.
'I was very much amused' is her summing up of an evening in the Royal box or, later, 'I was very very much amused', or 'I WAS VERY VERY MUCH AMUSED INDEED,' underlined three times.

4 Sew the leaf-shaped sequins around this centre to form the petals.

5 Sew more tiny metal beads down the stem and along the tendrils.

6 Sew a pink flower sequin under each tendril.

See! how she leans her cheek
upon her hand:
O! that I were a glove upon that hand,
That I might touch that cheek.

Romeo and Juliet
WILLIAM SHAKESPEARE
(1564–1616)

PICTURE MOUNT

*T*HIS PRETTY pressed flower picture mount is a lovely way to frame a special photograph and perhaps to remember a favourite garden in the height of summer. Pressed flowers are very fragile and it is more practical to use them to decorate the mount rather than the frame, so that they will be protected under glass.

MATERIALS

Selection of dried flowers and leaves
Ivory card mount (oval-shaped opening)
Rubber-based glue
Toothpicks for applying glue
Tweezers for handling flowers

1 Arrange the pressed flowers and leaves onto the card mount, emphasizing two diagonally opposite corners.

2 When you are happy with your design, starting at the top right-hand corner, dab small amounts of glue onto the card and press the flowers and leaves gently in place.

3 Repeat the process on the lower left-hand corner and allow the glue to dry thoroughly before mounting and framing your picture.

DÉCOUPAGE PICTURE FRAME

*D*ÉCOUPAGE BECAME a fashionable craze in the nineteenth century. The new developments in the printing industry made a greater variety of printed images and scraps available. These were avidly collected and pasted onto all manner of household items, such as frames, boxes and fire screens.

MATERIALS

Picture frame 23 × 28 cm (9 × 11 in), with
flat front 6 cm (2½ in) wide

Cream-coloured paint

Paintbrush

Scissors

Facsimile Victorian scraps of flowers

Wallpaper paste

Matt polyurethane varnish

Paintbrush for varnish

Sandpaper

1 Paint the frame with two coats of paint and allow to dry thoroughly.

2 Cut out the scraps and arrange them around the frame to help you decide on your final design.

3 Paste the frame and stick the scraps in place with the wallpaper paste. Press them firmly to expel any air bubbles. Allow the frame to dry.

4 Varnish with 3 coats of varnish, sanding the penultimate coat lightly to achieve a smooth finish. You can achieve an antique effect by adding a little burnt umber oil paint to the varnish.

GLASS FLOWERS

❧

*I*T WAS COMMON for Victorian homes to have wonderful arrangements of dried flowers in the living rooms. Garden flowers were picked at the height of the summer season and hung to dry in airy potting sheds. Roses, peonies, lavender and marigolds dry particularly well and were great favourites. This lovely arrangement is displayed beneath a glass dome, a practical and popular device, much favoured in Victorian times for preserving flowers and protecting them from household dust. In the language of flowers this dried arrangement would have signified 'Thou art all that is lovely' (rose), shame or bashfulness (peony) and grief (marigold). Perhaps the giver wished to make atonement for a careless remark.

MATERIALS

Cone-shaped oasis foam

Glass dome and stand

Scissors

Paper posy holder or doilie

Secateurs

Selection of dried flowers including hydrangeas, roses, peonies, lavender and marigolds

*F*lowers or aromatic plants require the smallest increase of heat beyond the temperature of the season, provided that season be genial: something more for rinds or roots and a greater heat for fruits: but this heat must not be carried to excess.

Enquire Within Upon Everything 1894

1 Make sure the oasis cone fits under the dome with enough room to accommodate the flowers. It can be trimmed with a sharp kitchen knife if necessary.

2 Cut the centre of a doilie or paper posy holder and push it over the oasis cone down to the base.

3 Cut the stems of the flowers to approximately 3 cm (1¼ in) and start arranging the larger flowers in a circle around the base of the cone.

4 Change the type of flower and the colour with each new circle, grading the flower sizes towards the top.

5 Fill the spaces between the large flowers such as the roses and peonies with tightly packed small bunches of lavender.

6 Finish the arrangement by choosing one perfect bud or flower to top the display. Fit the glass dome in place, and make any necessary adjustments to the flowers.

HOW TO DRY FLOWERS

*I*t is best to pick your chosen flowers on a dry, warm day just before they are in full bloom. This is because the blossoms continue to develop after they are picked and you want the petals to be secure. Strip off most of the leaves and gather them into small bunches of about 5 blooms, tying them loosely with string. Hang them upside down near the ceiling of a warm airy room; an old-fashioned airing cupboard is ideal. The largest flowers, such as peonies, are best hung singly as they can easily become distorted in a bunch. The flowers are ready for use when they are dry and papery to the touch with brittle stems. Store them in a dust-free environment until ready for use.

*I*t is the watchful eye of the mistress that keeps the home beautiful with the freshness of cleanliness and the calm of repose. Through her vigilance alone will the servants prove faithful in the performance of their duty.

Warne's Model Cookery 1869

BOOKMARK AND GIFT TAGS

*B*OOKS WERE treasured possessions in the Victorian household.
They were often expensive to buy and lavishly bound in gold embossed leather.
A small volume of poetry was a common addition to a lady's accessories, and
usually enclosed a pretty bookmark, often made by the lady herself.

BOOKMARK

MATERIALS

*Pressed flowers (viola and love-in-the-mist (Nigella))
and fern leaves*

Tweezers for handling flowers

Ivory card 16 × 4 cm (6¼ × 1½ in)

Rubber-based glue

Toothpick

Pale blue card 18 × 5 cm (7 × 2 in)

Scissors

Hole punch

30 cm (12 in) length of tartan ribbon, 2 cm (¾ in) wide

1 Arrange the flowers
centrally over the leaves
in a rectangular shape on
the prepared card. When
you are happy with your
design, carefully glue
the specimens in place,
dabbing the glue on
with the toothpick.

2 Stick onto pale blue
card, leaving a ½ cm
(¼ in) margin all round.
Cut a round tab at the
top of the bookmark,
then punch a hole in the
tab. Thread and knot the
ribbon through, then trim
the ends at an angle.

GIFT TAGS

*T*hese simple and delicate-looking gift tags,
decorated with single specimen flowers and
newly formed leaves, will make an enchanting
addition to a special present.

MATERIALS

Assorted scraps of recycled paper in pastel shades

Pencil

Scissors

Hole punch

Pressed specimen flowers (love-in-the-mist (Nigella))

Small new fern leaves

Rubber-based glue

Toothpick

Matching silk ribbon 1.5 cm (½ in) wide

1 Using small household
objects as templates such
as a matchbox or a lid,
draw around it onto the
coloured paper. Cut the
shape out and mount on
different-coloured paper,
leaving a small margin
around it. Remember
to leave a tab at one
end; punch a hole
in this.

2 Carefully glue the
specimen flowers in place,
then decorate with leaves.

3 Attach the silk ribbon
through the punched hole
and trim the ends.

For, to the noble mind,
Rich gifts wax poor when givers prove unkind.

Hamlet
WILLIAM SHAKESPEARE
(1564–1616)

POT POURRI

THE VICTORIANS delighted in the natural world and were keen gardeners. Herbs and flowers were grown for use in the kitchen and to decorate the house in summer and winter. Pretty bowls of homemade pot pourri were distributed throughout the house as an evocative and fragrant reminder of the garden at the height of summer.

ROSE AND LAVENDER POT POURRI

MATERIALS

Small bowl

5 ml (1 teaspoon) cinnamon powder

5 ml (1 teaspoon) whole cloves

2.5 ml (½ teaspoon) ground nutmeg

25 g (¾ oz) orris root powder

3 drops of lavender essential oil

3 drops of rose essential oil

Large bowl

500 ml (1 pt) mixed summer flowers, predominantly rose petals, buds and blooms

250 ml (½ pt) mixed lemon verbena, eau de Cologne mint, scented geranium leaves

30 g (1 oz) lavender

Dried flowers to decorate, including rosebuds, blooms and whole lavender

1 In a small bowl, mix together the spices, orris root powder and essential oils.

2 Rub the mixture between your fingers, making sure that the oil penetrates the mixture evenly.

3 In a large bowl mix together all the remaining ingredients, remembering to put aside some flowers for the surface decoration.

4 Add the mixture of orris root, spices and oils to the bowl of dry ingredients. Stir together to produce an evenly scented mixture.

5 Put this mixture into an airtight container and leave in a dark place for 3 weeks, occasionally shaking it. The longer you leave the mixture, the stronger the fragrance will become.

6 Remove the pot pourri from the airtight container and put into a pretty china bowl. Decorate the surface with flowers.

❧ SACHETS ❧

*T*hese exquisite little sachets filled with rose
and lavender pot pourri will delicately impart
their scent to your linen and simultaneously
help to keep the moths at bay.

MATERIALS

Scraps of printed fabric; cotton lawn or silk are most suitable

Scissors

Needle and matching thread

Pot pourri mixture

Pressed flowers of your choice

Fine net

Soft lace or crochet

*The smallest scraps of
lace, ribbon and pretty
fabrics can be made into
little bags that can then
be lightly stuffed with
highly scented pot pourri.
For a really unusual
decoration, lightly glue a
single pressed rosebud or
a group of pressed flowers
to the front of the sachet.
Protect by covering with a
fine net and finish by
adding a soft lace trim.*

*T*he maid of the Countess De Neige
Put others all in a rage.
What gave her such cachet
Were drawers full of sachets
Of lavender, rosemary and sage.

VICTORIAN LIMERICK

CRYSTALLIZED VIOLETS

CRYSTALLIZED VIOLETS surpass any other form of cake decoration and are traditionally used to decorate fine chocolate cakes. They look best arranged in a simple posy or as a circle of alternate leaves and flowers. You need to pick the violets and their heart-shaped leaves on a dry day. Keep them fresh in a jar of water while you are working since they wilt quickly.

MATERIALS

2 egg whites

Artist's paintbrush

Violet flowers and leaves

125 g (4 oz) caster sugar

Fine sieve

Greaseproof paper

Wire rack

1 Beat the egg whites until they are white and frothy. With the paintbrush paint each flower carefully with the egg white. Take care to paint the underside of the petals as well.

2 Holding the flower by its stalk, gently dust with the caster sugar, using a fine sieve. Turn the flower and dust the underside as well.

3 Lay a sheet of greaseproof paper onto the wire rack, and set the flowers down, making sure they do not touch.

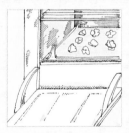

4 Put the rack of flowers to dry in a warm airy place. An airing cupboard is ideal; alternatively place the rack in a 'cool' oven with the door open until the flowers are dry.

5 To store the crystallized flowers, place them between layers of greaseproof paper in an airtight container.

TEAPOT STAND

Tea was an important occasion in the Victorian household, especially when guests were expected. The best china was used, along with the silver teapot, and delicious small sandwiches, tea cakes and fancies were served. The craft of découpage was extremely popular and this elegant teapot stand is an ideal small project to try.

MATERIALS

Round table mat	Prints of botanical illustrations	Rag
Fine sandpaper	Small scissors	Burnt umber oil paint
Mauve paint	Wallpaper paste	Polyurethane varnish
Paintbrush	Crackle varnish	Brush for varnish

1 Sand the surface of the table mat to provide a key for the paint.

2 Paint with 2 coats of mauve paint.

3 Carefully cut out the botanical illustrations with the small scissors.

4 When you have decided where to lay the prints, apply paste to the mat and stick them down, easing out any trapped air bubbles with your fingers.

5 Allow to dry and apply the crackle glaze following the maker's instructions. The second coat may be dried with a hair dryer.

6 Rub the burnt umber oil paint into the crackles with the rag, then wipe off the excess with a clean rag. Allow the teapot stand to dry and apply at least 5 coats of polyurethane varnish. For a really smooth finish, lightly sand the penultimate coat.

SHELL BOXES

$\mathcal{T}$HE VICTORIANS had a passion for collecting shells, and also seaweed, which was pressed and arranged into albums. It is still possible to find stunning examples of 'the sailor's Valentine' – framed pictures of exquisite tiny shells arranged into a 'shell mosaic'. These little boxes with their pearly shell decorations will not fail to grace any dressing table.

$\mathcal{H}$e had 42 boxes all carefully packed,
With his name painted clearly on each
But, since he omitted to mention the fact,
They were all left behind on the beach.

The Hunting of the Snark
LEWIS CARROLL 1832–98

MATERIALS

Small wooden boxes – heart-shaped, rectangular or oval

Fine sandpaper

Dusty pink paint

Gilt cream

Rag

PVA glue

Selection of small shells including petal-shaped shells

Tweezers

Paper lace

1 Lightly sand the box and its lid with fine sandpaper. Apply 2 coats of paint. Allow to dry.

2 Lightly rub the gilt cream over the sides of the box and the edge of the lid. Polish with a clean rag.

3 Glue a pearly spiral shell onto the centre of the box lid.

4 Glue petal-shaped shells around the central shell to make a flower shape.

$\mathcal{Y}$ou could also try arranging shells as a frame around a pretty Victorian scrap pasted to the lid of a box.

Do not keep the alabaster boxes of your love and tenderness sealed up until your friends are dead. Fill their lives with sweetness. Speak approving cheering words while their hearts can be thrilled by them.

HENRY WARD BEECHER 1831–87

5 *Surround the flower with tightly packed tiny pearly shells. Finish off the design with 2 rows of contrasting shells, following the edge of the lid.*

6 *Finish by gluing paper lace around the base and bottom edge of the box.*

And the hyacinth purple, and white and blue,
Which flung from its bells a sweet peal anew
Of music so delicate, soft and intense,
It was felt like an odour within the sense.

From *Spring Flowers*
PERCY BYSSHE SHELLEY
(1792–1822)

HYACINTHS AND GARLANDS

WHO CAN resist the beauty and heady perfume of a hyacinth grown indoors, an early messenger of spring? A variety of spring bulbs were prepared by the gardener to bring into the Victorian house to flower early in the year. Among the most popular, the strongly perfumed hyacinth was grown in specially designed glasses. Later in the year scented garlands, made from flowers fresh from the garden, were used to decorate the home on festive occasions.

GARLAND

*F*or a special occasion drape this lovely scented garland over a picture, fireplace or ornamental mirror frame.

MATERIALS

Ball of string

Assortment of flowers and leaves, according to season

Reel of florists' wire

1 m (3 ft) of matching wired ribbon.

1 Tie a loop at each end of a piece of string 80 cm (32 in) long.

2 Make small bunches of leaves and flowers. Lay them onto the string and bind them on with florists' wire. Add more bunches, each one overlapping the previous bunch. Make sure the garland is completely covered, both front and back.

3 Add a ribbon bow at each end, and hang a small bunch of leaves and flowers from behind the bows.

O, Brignal banks are wild and fair,
And Greta woods are green,
And you may gather garlands there
Would grace a summer queen.

Rokeby
SIR WALTER SCOTT (1771–1832)

STENCILLED NOTEBOOK

*T*HE VICTORIANS took an enthusiastic interest in botany, and ferns had a particular appeal to their romantic notions since they grew in wild and exotic places. Keen collectors assembled fern albums, even displaying living examples in specially designed containers. The intricate feathery fronds of the fern create a beautiful design when used as a stencil.

MATERIALS

Notebook with hard cover

Newspaper

Spray paint – bright green, dark green and brown

Pressed ferns

Scissors

Burnt umber oil paint

Polyurethane varnish

Brush

Fine sandpaper

1 Place the book on newspaper and spray the front and back with the bright green paint.

2 When the paint has dried, spray over very lightly with darker green paint to give a mottled effect.

*O*f all the needs a book has the chief need is that it be readable.

Autobiography
ANTHONY TROLLOPE
(1815–82

3 Cut the fern specimens to fit the size of the book and lay them onto the cover quite flat. Spray carefully with the brown paint, just going over the edges slightly to create an outline.

4 Remove the ferns and repeat on the back of the book.

5 Mix a small amount of burnt umber oil into some varnish, and apply 3 coats, or more if the cover of the book is at all absorbent. Sand the penultimate coat lightly to achieve a smooth finish.

A birdie with a yellow bill
Hopped upon the window-sill,
Cocked his shining eye and said,
'Ain't you 'shamed you sleepy head?'

Time to Rise
ROBERT LOUIS STEVENSON
(1850–94)

HERB PILLOW

*T*HE VICTORIANS had an extensive knowledge of the therapeutic uses of fragrant herbs and flowers. Advice abounded on the importance of the bedroom arrangements, which had to be spacious, lofty, well ventilated and uninhabited during the day, and many ills were blamed on the lack of a sound night's sleep. Fresh flowers or potted plants were never placed in a bedroom as they were thought to be injurious to the health at night. This pretty pillow stuffed with sleep-inducing herbs will sweeten the night air.

MATERIALS

50 cm (20 in) calico

Needle

Thread

Pins

750 ml (1½ pt) mixed lime blossom, hops and jasmine flowers

50 cm (20 in) printed Victorian pattern cotton

1.5 m (3 ft) matching fringed braid

*T*o make a Victorian bed was neither a short nor a simple task. There were usually three mattresses. The heavy bottom mattress, stuffed with straw, was turned only once a week; the middle mattress, made of wool or horsehair, was turned daily; and the feather mattress on top had to be shaken, pummelled, smacked and turned every day until it was as light and puffed as a soufflé.

Life Below Stairs
FRANK E. HUGGETT

1 Cut two pieces of calico 23 × 27 cm (9 × 11 in). Sew up three sides to make a bag and turn inside out.

2 Mix the herbs together and lightly stuff them into the bag.

3 Neatly sew up the open end, and roughly tack across the bag to keep the herbs in place.

4 Cut two pieces of printed fabric. With right sides together sew around three sides, then turn the right way round.

5 Push the calico pillow inside the cotton case, and sew up the open end.

6 Sew matching braid around the edge of the pillow, making sure the braid lies flat around the corners. Finish off neatly.

DRIED FLOWERS

❦

THE WELL-PLANNED Victorian kitchen garden included beds of flowers grown specifically for cutting. These were used for fresh flower arrangements during the summer for the parlour and dining room. Bunches were hung up to dry in airy potting sheds, kitchens or attics for use in dried-flower displays, the making of fragrant pot pourris, scented sachets and therapeutic herb pillows. Most garden flowers are suitable for drying and will keep their colour well if the correct procedure is followed.

1 Pick the flowers on a dry, warm day. Select flowers that are freshly opened or still in bud. Lay them carefully in a garden tray.

2 Remove some of the leaves from the stems to encourage quicker drying. Pick the thorns off the rose stems to protect your fingers later on.

3 Put approximately 8 stems together in a loose bunch. Try to keep the flowerheads as loose as possible.

4 Tie the bunches together with gardener's twine and suspend from a line stretched across a room.

❧ TO DRY FLOWERS IN SILICA GEL ❧

*U*SE SILICA GEL to dry special flowers singly. It is a magical process. The crystals have a powerful desiccating effect and so you can dry flowers in a very short time. It has the advantage of preserving the colour and form of the bloom perfectly.

Flowers particularly suitable for drying are larkspur, roses, achillea, African marigolds, cornflowers, delphiniums, lavender, meadowsweet, astilbes, grasses, love-in-the-mist and honesty.

MATERIALS

2 kg (4¹/₂ lb) silica gel

Deep-sided baking tray

Flowerheads – roses, pansies, peonies etc.

Aluminium foil to cover tray

1 Put a layer of silica gel in the bottom of the baking tray. Take care not to breathe in the dust of the silica gel.

2 Lay the flowers carefully into the silica and gently sift more gel over the flowerheads to fill in the spaces between the petals.

3 Continue building up layers of flowers and silica gel. Cover with foil and leave for up to a week. Store the silica gel in an airtight container and wash your hands after use.

4 Remove the flowers carefully from the silica gel. They will be perfectly dried in form and colour and can be used to stunning effect in floral arrangements.

INDEX

—A—

Accessories 22
Achillea 43
Albums 10, 38
Astilbes 43

—B—

Ballet 22
Baskets 18
Beaded gloves 10, 22–3
Beads
    glass 16
    metal 22
Bedrooms 41
Beecher, Henry 35
Bookmark and gift tags 28
Books 10, 38
Botany 10, 38
Boxes
    découpage 25
    shell 34–6
Braid 41
Bulbs 37

—C—

Cakes, chocolate 11, 32
Calico 41
Candles 12–13
Card 16, 18, 19, 28
    mount 24
    pressed flower 18–20
Carol service 13
Carroll, Lewis 34
Caster sugar 11, 32
Chalk 22
Chocolate cakes 11, 32
Cinnamon 30
Cistus 19
Cloves 30
Coal dust 11
Cornflowers 14, 43
Craft knives 16
Cranesbill 19
Crystallized violets 11, 32

—D—

Daisies 19
Découpage
    picture frame 25
    teapot stand 33
Delphiniums 43
Doilies 19, 26
Domes, glass 11, 26, 27
Drying flowers 27, 42–3

—E—

Egg white 11, 32
Embroidery 10
Essential oils 30

—F—

Ferns 11, 12, 16, 18, 28, 38
Feverfew 14
Fire screens 25
Florist's wire 14, 37
Flowers
    drying 27, 42–3
    glass 26–7
    language of 14, 26
    pressing 11, 12, 16
Frame 11, 18, 25

—G—

Gardens 10, 30, 42
Garlands 37
Gaskell, Elizabeth 13
Geraniums 12, 19, 30
Gift tags 28–9
Glass
    beads 16
    domes 11, 26, 27
    flowers 26–7
Gloves, beaded 10, 22–3
Grasses 43
Greaseproof paper 32
Growing pansies 14

—H—

Hearts 16–17
Herbs 30
    pillows 41, 42
    Tussie Mussie 14
Hole punches 28

Honesty 43
Huggett, Frank E. 41
Hyacinths 36, 37
Hydrangeas 12

—J—

Jasmine 41
Journals 10, 22

—K—

King, Jonathan 16

—L—

Lace 31
Ladysmocks 19
Lampshades 10, 21
Language of love 14, 26
Larkspur 43
Lavender 12, 30, 31, 43
Leafy lampshade 21
Leaves, skeletonizing 10, 21
Lemon verbena 30
Lime blossom 41
Love
    language of 14, 26
    notes 17
Love-in-a-mist 28, 43

—M—

Magnolias 21
Marigolds 14, 26, 43
Mattresses 41
Meadowsweet 43
Metal beads 22
Mint 30
Mosaics 34
Moths 31

—N—

Needles 22, 31, 41
Net 31
Newspaper 38
Nigella 28
Notebook, stencilled 11, 38–40
Nutmeg 30

—O—

Oasis foam 26
Opera 22
Orris root 30

—P—

Paint 25, 33, 34, 38
Pansies 12, 14–15, 43
Paper 16, 17, 18, 19
Paper glue 17, 19
Paper lace 34
Paraffin wax 12, 13
Pencils 16, 19, 28
Penmanship 10
Peonies 26, 43
Photocopiers 17
Picture,
    frames 11, 18, 25
    mount, 24
    pressed flower 11, 18–20, 24
Pillows, herb 41, 42
Pinking shears 16
Pinks 14
Pins 41
Posy holder 26
Pot pourri 30–1
Potentillas 12, 19
Pressed flowers
    card and picture 11, 18–20
    picture mount 24
    preparing 10, 11, 12, 16
Primroses 12
PVA glue 34

—R—

Ribbon 16, 17, 19, 28, 37
Rosebay willow herb 19
Rosemary 14, 31
Roses 14, 26, 43
Rubber-based glue 16, 18, 19, 21, 24, 28

—S—

Sachets, pot pourri 31
Sage 31
Sandpaper 25, 33, 34, 38
Santolina 14

Scott, Walter 37
Secateurs 26
Seed, growing pansies from 14
Sequins 10, 22
Shakespeare, William 19, 23, 29
Shell boxes 34–6
Shelley, Percy Bysshe 36
Sieve 32
Silica gel 43
Skeletonizing leaves 10, 21
Statice 19
Stencilled notebook 11, 38–40
Stevenson, Robert L. 40
String 37
Sugar 11, 32
Swansdown 16

—T—

Table mat 33
Tallow candles 12
Tea 17, 33
Teapot stand 33
Thread 22, 31, 41
Tinsel 16
Toothpicks 16, 19, 24, 28
Trollope, Anthony 38
Tussie Mussie 14
Tweezers 18, 19, 24, 28, 34

—V—

Valentines 11, 16, 34
Varnish 25, 33, 38
Verse 10
Victoria, Queen 22
Violas 14, 28
Violets 14–15, 19
    crystallized 11, 32
Valentines 16

—W—

Wallpaper paste 25, 33
Watercolours 10
Wax candles 12
Willow 21
Wordsworth, William 15

ACKNOWLEDGEMENTS

The author would like to give very special
thanks to Heini Schneebeli for his care and attention
to detail in taking the really lovely photographs in
this book. And to all my good friends who have
happily lent me beautiful objects from their own
homes: Raynes Minns, Duffy Ayers, Anthea
Sieveking, Marion Manheimer, Mary Port and Dulcie
Beilin Morel; to Gloria Nichol for her constant
encouragement; and to Roger Vlitos for advice on
the fern stencilled notebook on pages 38–9. Special
thanks to Anna Bentinck for her invaluable help
with finding the original Victorian material.
The Victorian limerick on page 31 comes
from the author's own collection; Life Below Stairs,
Frank E. Huggett (1977), quoted on page 41,
is published by John Murray Ltd. Dried flowers
supplied by Chattels, 53 Chalk Farm Road, London
NW1 8AN (mail order tel. 0171 267 0877).

Very special thanks to my two children,
Hannah and Raphael, and to Teo Spurring, who
have been so patient, understanding and supportive
during the production of this book.